Art of Wine Making Business Startup

How to Start a Million Dollar Success from Home

BY

Alberto Ricci

Published by:

Valley Of Joy Publishing Press
P.O. Box 966
Semmes, Alabama 36575

Cover & Interior designed

By

Ruby Romano

First Edition

TABLE OF CONTENTS

PART – 1

HOW TO START MAKING WINE

INTRODUCTION

IF you are reading this book, then you are probably thinking about getting into the world of wine-making. I can't say that I blame you. Wine-making is a fun activity that is not only affordable to get into but could also be profitable if you just put in your best effort into the process.

I started making wine about 14 years back, but it wasn't necessarily something that I expected I would be doing for a while. I started making my wine out of curiosity.

I was curious as to how I could prepare wine myself. I have had one too many bad experiences with wine over the years. It seems as though there are far too many winemakers out there who don't understand what people want out of their wines.

There are just far too many wines out there that are anything but appealing. Some are far too bitter and others just feel watery or syrupy. Others just have terrible odors that only make them worse.

The frustration I have had with wines over the years got me thinking – what if I tried to make wine myself? Surely I could do somewhat better than all those other people who make wine if I just put in a good amount of effort into the process.

It was a crazy idea, but I figured that every smart idea in the world starts out of something crazy, right?

I also figured it would be fun to see just what types of wine I could produce. I have seen so many brands pop up selling wines of all sorts. I assume they all run their vineyards with separate sections for red and white wine. But what could I do to produce something distinctive and unique?

I had to set up a plan for making my wine. I looked around and found as much information as I could about making wine. I focused on how the individual ingredients for wine work while also looking into the proper conditions for making wine.

I did not want to spend lots of money on the process either. It is not like I was going to sell that wine to people.

I especially had to look for the right materials for making the wine. I didn't want to use just any containers for storing it. I had to find great items that were sturdy, secure and easy to use.

It took a while for me to get it all right but after a few months and a few hundred dollars, I finally started making my wine. The results were amazing.

I found that making wine is easy by using the right mix of ingredients and planning the fermentation process well. Best of all, that wine could be as good as or even better than what you would find on the open market.

Eventually, I started making even more wine. Today I have my small operation where I sell wines to local businesses and restaurants in my area. I had to go through a few legal points to make it work while getting the word out about your efforts too, but it was worthwhile in the end.

I hope to expand my reach a little further down the road. I have even looked into various types of grapes for different wines to see which ones turn out the best. After all, it never hurts to try out a variety of wines.

Best of all, this whole thing started without too much of an investment. It is amazing as to how you could make your wine at home without having to throw thousands of dollars into the process like what so many other people tend to do.

I decided to write this guide to help you understand how you can make your wine at home. This guide includes all the points you need to know about making wine.

The information in this guide is based on my experience with wine. If it can work for me then surely it will do the same for you.

You will learn many of the ins and outs that come with making wine through this guide. These include points like:

- What you require for making wine
- Understanding the different types of wine
- Legal points relating to making wine
- Getting the equipment for winemaking safe and ready for use
- The fermentation process
- Storing wine properly
- Selling your wine; this includes points on the legal aspects of doing so

Best of all, you will find that it is not all that expensive for you to start making wine. It only costs a few hundred dollars when you begin although your experience might vary.

With all this in mind, let us get started with a look at how you can make your wine at home.

CHAPTER 1 - WHY START MAKING WINE?

WHY would you make your wine? There are plenty of wine stores out there that are selling wine that people make for your enjoyment. There are so many options out there that you are certainly bound to find something interesting and worthy of your time.

That is what I thought when I started making wine. I figured that there would not be all that much of a difference between the wine I make and whatever is out there right now. But as it turns out, there are many good reasons why you should make your wine.

AFFORDABLE TO DO

It is not all that expensive for you to produce your wine provided that you have the appropriate materials on hand of the process. If anything, it could cost anywhere from $3 to $5 per bottle after you have the materials on hand and the grapes and other ingredients necessary.

The initial investment for your wine-making plans will pay off as it does not cost much to make wine when you prepare everything. If anything, you don't have to spend more than a few hundred dollars to get all the stuff you need for wine-making.

You do have the option to move on to some more advanced items for your wine-making efforts like fancy wooden barrels. That would cost an extra bit of money for you to get though. It would especially be best if you were a little more experienced with your winemaking efforts.

A RELAXING ACTIVITY

Wine-making is also a very relaxing and rewarding activity to get into. As you make your wine, you will enjoy the leisurely pace that comes with the process.

It does take a while for wine to be ready. But as you prepare your wine, you will see that you're having a fun time enjoying the process.

Marvel at how well grapes grow and how they ferment over time. See how the color of the wine changes based on the skins you use. Notice the appealing scent of the wine as it comes along.

Wine is ideal when you savor it slowly. As you make your wine, you will have the opportunity to try it out and experience some of the tones and scents that come with your production. Experience the beauty of the wine as you taste it; no two glasses are ever truly alike.

A SOCIAL ACTIVITY

Wine-making is also fun for how it brings people together. When you make your wine, you are inviting other people to come along and enjoy what you are producing. Bringing other people you know into the fray is always a good idea. Wine is a fine drink groups of people enjoy.

You could even find a wine-making community in your area to get into. Many communities entail groups that offer support for one another's wine-making needs. People often set up events where they exchange and taste wines or offer tips with one another over how well wines can be made. Just imagine the friendships you can develop when you make wines with other people.

FUN TO EXPERIMENT

As you will notice in this guide, there are many types of wines you could make in your home. The various types of grapes that you might use are varied, for instance. Feel free to test many of them out to see what fits in with your demands for a quality wine.

If anything, you could probably make your unusual or intriguing flavors when making your wines. Just because people talk all the time about red and white wines and all that stuff doesn't mean you need to stick with the standards.

The guidelines in this book are simply points to look into when figuring out ways to make wine in your home. You have the right to play around with the rules of winemaking in any way you see fit.

CHAPTER 2 - LEGALITY POINTS

THE thrill surrounding making your wine is certainly something. But since this entails alcohol, you will be subject to specific laws relating to how you can make wine. You must follow all proper rules for making wine, so you will enjoy your experience without being at risk of legal harm.

Note: The following laws are primarily for people in the United States. The laws in your country may vary although some aspects of American law may carry over to your country.

WHO IS IT FOR?

To start, there are rules over who you can serve your wine to. In most places, you would have the right serve your wine to people in your household. These include family members and friends who come over provided they are of the legal drinking age.

In most states, you would only be allowed to make wine for your own use without selling it. However, you could apply for a permit to sell your wine to people outside your home. This would work provided that you file the appropriate paperwork and take care of other plans relating to getting your wine ready for sale. You will learn more about how to legally sell your wine later in this guide.

How Much Can You Prepare?

There are limits regarding how much wine you can produce and have in your home at a given time. United States law, according to Public Law 95-458 established in 1978, says that you can only produce up to 200 gallons of wine in a year if there are two or more adults in the household or up to 100 gallons if there is only one adult.

The rules may vary based on where you are. Talk with local government entities, particularly alcohol control boards, in your state to learn more about what can be done where you live.

Where Are the Resources From?

The wines and other ingredients that you use might have to come from a specific place if you are to legally make your wine. For example, in North Carolina people must use grapes, grain extracts and other items that come from that particular state.

Contact a local government office in your area to get specifics on what you can do for making wine in your home. You might have limits as to what grapes or other edible materials you could use in the process.

AGE POINTS

Did you know that in the United States you could be 18 years of age and brew wine? I know this is pretty interesting to its right. Then again, I am willing to bet you are at least 21 years of age if you are reading this book right now. Or at least I hope you are of that age.

Still, I would strongly encourage people who are from 18 to 21 years of age to avoid brewing their wines. You would still be in possession of alcohol or at an increased likelihood to consume the alcohol at that age. Serving to minors is obviously illegal.

The best tip is to create a secure space for making wine that people will not easily get into. Keep a series of locks on a door or other storage spot. Do not let just anyone get into your wine-making operation.

AVOID DISTILLING

You must allow your grapes to ferment but that should be it. You cannot engage in distilling in your home.

Distilling refers to a process where fruits and other items that have fermented are distilled. That is, you are vaporizing the fermented liquid and then condensing it by cooling off the vapor. At that point, you would collect the vaporized liquid.

This process is used to produce hard liquor. It is a type of liquor much more powerful than wine as its alcohol by volume content is higher.

Distilling is completely illegal for you to do in your home. Besides, the distilling process should work through expert liquor companies that have enough experience for handling this setup.

Be certain you look at the rules relating to making wine and what you can get out of the process. Do not think just once when getting the most out of your wine. Think carefully about how well your wine may be produced.

CHAPTER 3 - TYPES OF WINES YOU CAN MAKE

WHEN you read a wine list at a restaurant or go shopping for wine at a local retailer, you might see those wines divided up by kind. One section features white wines while another has red ones.

One of the greatest parts of wine is that it is available in a variety of styles. Naturally, the most common types of wines that you could find are red and white wine.

Figuring out the type of wine you want can make a real difference. Find wine that you know you will enjoy making. Choose something that has a good flavor or tone to it. You will be impressed at how well-made wine can be.

UNDERSTANDING THE DIFFERENCE BETWEEN RED AND WHITE WINE

On the surface, red and white wine is different in terms of their appearances. But what makes the two of them so different from each other?

Such wines are made based on the grapes that you choose. Different types of grapes are responsible for producing wines in various forms. But the individual features of these wines are different from one another.

The main point is that red wine has been in contact with the skins of the grapes used in its production. White wine has not been in such contact.

The tannins within your wine make a huge impact on what you will get out of it. These compounds typically cause a wine to feel dry.

Such tannins are found in the skins, seeds and stems in your grapes. They will release into your wine as such compounds are stuck inside the juice being fermented. Your wine will have a darker appearance to it when the tannins have been soaking in the wine for a longer period.

These tannins often cause your wine to have a bolder taste. This creates something a little more intense, a point that makes red wine better when consuming fleshier and meatier foods.

With these points in mind, here are a few points to see regarding what makes red and white wine different from one another:

Red Wine	White Wine
Skins of grapes are in contact with the grape juice as it ferments	Grape skins are removed before the fermentation begins
Feature berry-like flavors or tones	More of a mineral flavor
Herbal or tobacco-like secondary tones can occur	Oily or nutty secondary tones develop
Tannins allow red wines to age longer	Tannins are not a factor
Has more of a smooth texture	Features a crisp and tart-like texture
Fleshier foods pair well with red wine	White wine is ideal for lighter foods with less of a texture
Tannins cause a dry feeling	Fewer tannins keep the wine from feeling too dry

Red and white wines are distinct. Look at what makes each option different so you have a good idea of what is ideal for your wine-making plans.

SPECIFIC RED WINES

You could start by making one of many kinds of red wine in your home. The type of wine you would produce varies based on the particular grapes you order. A grape farmer should provide you with information on the particular type of grape you have ordered and how well it can support a good wine.

The great thing about red wine is that it has a rich body that takes a bit to consume. This is great as the best wines are ones that take a while for you to enjoy. You should have time to savor the wine you take in and have fun with it.

Of course, there is the problem of red wine creating some huge stains. It is tough to clean out red wine from any surface it gets on. The color of the wine is just too dense.

That is just an appealing part of the character surrounding red wine. With this kind of wine, you will have something that looks beautiful and intriguing. Just make sure you watch for how you consume it and that you don't try having it over a fancy rug.

Here are a few of the more commonplace red wines that you might find. Each requires its specific growing temperature and goes well with specific foods:

Type of Red Wine	Features	Growing Temperature (in F)	What It Pairs With
Shiraz (syrah)	Hearty and spicy, deep flavor and tone	63-68	Most meats

Merlot	Easier to drink, has a berry-like tone	63-66	No specific; highly versatile
Cabernet sauvignon	Full-bodied with a few peppery tones	63-67	Red meat
Malbec	Easier to drink	62-66	Most meat-based entrees
Pinot noir	Very smooth	55-60	Chicken, lamb and salmon
Zinfandel	Sweet and peppery	64-70	Meats and most Italian foods
Sangiovese	Light in tone	63-67	Various Italian foods

SPECIFIC WHITE WINES

White wines are worth looking into as well. Some people find them easier to make because they don't require you to stick the seeds, stems or skins inside the juice while you are fermenting it.

White wine is made with a light taste and goes down with relative ease. This ensures you don't have any problems with consuming it. You might have an easier time consuming white wine if you aren't careful.

White wine does have kind of a yellowish tint to it when you look at it in the right light. That is just a natural feature of the wine though.

Let us look at a few of these wines. As you will notice, these white wines have grapes that grow based on cooler conditions.

Type of White Wine	Features	Growing Temperature (in F)	What It Pairs With
Chardonnay	Wide-bodied with a sparkling tone	45-55	Fish and chicken
Sauvignon blanc	Peppery and grassy tone with some smoky effects	50-55	Seafood and salads
Moscato	Fruity and sweet	48-52	With some desserts but best on its own

Pinot Grigio	Aromatic and fruity	50-55	Varied; highly versatile
Riesling	Light in tone with an apple-like flavor	48-58	Fish and chicken

The boldest wines tend to grow in warmer conditions. Lighter wines are best for cooler climates. Check on how well you can grow grapes for wines where you live.

WHAT ABOUT ROSE WINE?

Rose wines are also possible. Such a wine is right in the middle between red and white. It is distinguished by its light appearance.

This would require a bit of effort on your part. You would have to get black-skinned grapes and have skins exposed with the juice for a brief period. One day is typically enough. The color will be more intense if the skins are left in for a longer amount.

Some rose wine products might include a few additional fruits added to the mix. The strawberry and raspberry may be added into the wine to create a light pink tone and even a bit of extra flavor. This could be interesting and worth looking into when you're trying to have something enjoyable.

Feel free to experiment with as many types of wine as you want. The great thing about the world of wine is that it is very diverse and appealing. You are bound to find something great when looking around and choosing wines that you know fit in perfectly with your wine-making plans.

CHAPTER 4 - TIMING POINTS

YOU have probably heard that saying about old wine being better. Maybe you recall those old television commercials where Orson Welles tells you to never buy wine before its time...when he isn't drunk off of the product that is.

Well, it is true that it takes a while for wine to be ready. The fermentation and aging process takes a while. The final product is certainly worthwhile.

THE GENERAL FERMENTATION PROCESS

There are no specific timetables as to how long you have to wait for your grape plants to ferment properly. It takes around 10 to 15 days for wine to ferment at the least. You then need another week for the wine to clear up after it ferments so it will not weaken quickly.

The fermentation process should be undisturbed for the most part. The wine has to age properly while the yeast you apply into the mix moves through well enough. I'll talk a little more about the yeast later on in this guide by the way.

The wine would have to age for a few weeks for the best results. You could technically consume the wine right then and there, but it is best to wait a month or two for the wine to fully mature and have a bolder and more detailed flavor.

Everything must be fully secured in containers to ensure nothing spoils or ages prematurely. You will learn more about how to use proper containers a little later on in this guide.

You don't need fancy containers for your wines either. Be certain that you look at what is available so you have materials that are easy to support.

HOW LONG CAN WINE LAST FOR?

Wine can last for a good period if prepared right and stored properly.

Here are a few points for how long wine could last for on average:

Type of Wine	Average Lifespan
Bottled white wine	1 to 2 years, possibly longer if kept in a cool climate
Bottled red wine	2 to 3 years, longer if kept in the dark
Wine juice box	1 year; it must be insulated properly
Opened bottle of white wine	1 to 3 days
Opened bottle of red wine	1 week
Opened box of wine	6 to 9 months

Additional information on storing your wine so it can last long will be covered in a later chapter.

But What About the Old Ones?

It is true that there are lots of old bottles of wine out there. These include bottles that are several years in age. Wine enthusiasts argue that the oldest wines around are the most appealing and valuable because of how they have been aged to perfection. There's a reason why in 1997 someone paid more than $100,000 to get a Chateau Mouton Rothschild wine bottle from 1945.

But your efforts in making such wines will not entail trying to make ones that will last for generations. The truth is that it takes decades for you to make a fine wine.

A "fine wine" is one which comes from a professional vineyard that has been around for generations and has an established a series of grape plants and an extensive fermentation center. More importantly, such wine is one heralded by experts in the field who taste them regularly to determine which ones are the most valuable.

I would love to make fine wines myself but those wines probably would not get anywhere near that status until long after I am dead. I bet other people who started famous wineries around the world knew that just as well when they started their operations.

But still, the wines that are produced today are made to be just as appealing even if they aren't going to last as long. The taste of your wine is influenced by not only time but also by the quality of your grapes.

In short, don't stress out and try to make something that would last for years. Be willing just to try and produce something you know is great for now. Besides, practice always makes perfect.

GETTING PLANTS READY

While you could always use pre-existing grapes to produce your wines, you might also have a desire to get your wine plants ready. It could take a while for you to plant and prepare such plants though.

Your efforts for planning and ordering vines and getting the soil ready for them will take a while. It could take months for grapes to grow off of a fresh vine.

Fortunately, you will have an infinite supply of grapes if you take care of your plants well enough.

Those plants will grow quickly and effortlessly when treated right.

Create an open space for your plants as well. The plants should be in spots where they can expand while having enough room for growth.

Your grape plant is not going to expand in terms of ground cover. It does grow based on how many grapes are produced over time. The plant climbs upward and becomes a little stronger after a while. This adds a nice design that offers a more relaxed body.

Be ready to spend a good amount with your wine. It always takes a while to make wine but no good thing comes without effort.

CHAPTER 5 - WHAT YOU NEED FIRST

N OW it is time for us to discuss what you would require for getting the most out of your wine-making plans. Let us start by looking at what you would require out of the process at the start.

The key point about these items is that they will provide you with a cheap solution for preparing wine. I am not asking you to blow loads of money on the process. After all, the title of this book does say that the process is all about working while on a budget.

PROPER CONTAINERS

I want to start by looking at how you are will store your wine. You must keep your wine protected and in a secure series of containers. The problem though is that you have to get everything sized properly while organizing individual items based on their overall functions. It is not always easy to do this but it will not be too tough to get the most out of your work when you look at how you could set up a quality container.

Start by getting the correct containers ready for your wine. Various types of containers can be used in the process including plastic options.

You could even get some wooden barrels if desired. These are often used by professional wine makers who want to add some woodsy tones to their wines. These also ensure that the wine is kept in a dark space as it is being prepared.

But for budget purposes, it is best to use glass containers. Glass jars are perfect for how they are easy to clean off and prepare.

You would require the following two types of jars

1. A separate space for getting your grapes into while mixing other ingredients inside it
2. A carboy for securing the wine; this is where your wine will be stored in for weeks on end

You could have as many of these two types of jars as you want. The key is to have enough to where you can support the individual materials you wish to produce.

The cost associated with glass jars can vary. A one-gallon jar or jug may go for about $15 to $20. A five-gallon carboy bottle would go for $30 to $50.

The carboy is a great option for wine-making. This glass container features a small neck. It keeps the air inside the container under control and supports a stopper to keep excess oxygen from getting in there. This allows the yeast to convert the grape sugar into alcohol, thus giving you the wine you want.

But when finding glass, you must look for the following points:

- The glass materials you get must be fully new. They should not have been used for preparing other foods as some bits from those items could run off into your wine and ruin it. This is especially important if anything salty or sour like pickles were inside a glass container.

- Each container must be perfectly intact. Anything with even the slightly chip or crack might be risky.

- Look for something with a darker body. A glass jar with a brownish or blue-tinted body is great as it keeps the light that might get into the jar from being too strong. Of course, you should still keep the jar in a dark space; the tint of the glass just makes it a little easier for the wine to stay protected.

Just look at how well glass works for your needs. You might be surprised at how well glass works as it not only insulates the wine well but also offers a safe space for your needs.

COULD A PLASTIC FERMENTER WORK?

A plastic fermenter could be appealing. Such a unit would cost around $30 for a five-gallon size. This should have a secure space with enough room for your wine.

But even with that, plastic is not necessarily perfect. The problem with plastic materials is that sometimes they have chemical compounds used to keep their bodies intact.

Check the bottom of any plastic container if you wish to go down that route. See that it has a #1 PET or #2 HDPE label on it. These two plastic forms are the only ones safe for wine-making. Any other option might allow oxygen to sneak into the wine. A #7 plastic would be even worse as it is more likely to be made with chemical compounds.

WHAT ABOUT WOOD?

Oak barrels and other wooden containers are staples in the massive cellars and brewing stations professional wine makers have today. Such large-scale wineries use wood because the material creates a fully insulated space for fermentation and storage. Wood also produces a more natural-feeling tone into the wine, thus creating a more detailed flavor.

However, a wooden barrel is not necessarily the most affordable thing for you to have. It would cost a few hundred dollars for you to get a single wooden barrel. This would entail a new barrel that has not been used for anything else and would be safe to handle.

Also, most wooden barrels tend to be relatively large in size. You would be hard-pressed to find a barrel that features less than ten gallons of room. Simply put, wooden barrels are better suited for more advanced operations when you have gotten used to the process of making wine.

Therefore, sticking with glass containers is the best thing to do. Wood is made for professionals and those who are highly successful and have large amounts of money to work with.

A PLASTIC TUBE

A siphoning tube must be applied in the next part. This tube transfers the wine from the main mixing jar into the carboy bottle.

The tube may come with a slight filter or strainer. Such a piece keeps the pulp or skins from your original mixing jar from getting into the carboy. Your final product will be smooth and crisp without any chunks or bits in the way provided you secure it well enough.

Such a tube requires a simple process for it to work:

1. You would have to place the carboy at a spot lower than the mixing jar.

2. As you insert the tube into the mixing jar, you must move it up and down. This draws out the wine.

3. The pressure generated causes the wine to move into the carboy provided that the tube has been positioned there.

This is a simple process that keeps the wine moving between containers. It is simple and easy to follow.

A siphon tube can be acquired for around $10. Such a tube will go for about five to eight feet. Make sure that tube is thick and flexible.

See that you have a cap that allows you to stick a tube into the main bottle so it can move the wine into the carboy. It must be flexible enough to move through well while still allowing wine to move through without having lots of excess air get in the way.

On a related note, you could find an automatic siphon tube that produces an up-and-down motion. The plastic material uses a small switch that triggers the function. The convenience of such a tool does cost you a little extra though as you would have to spend a few dollars more for such a model.

AIRLOCK AND STOPPER

An airlock is the next part to into the mix. An airlock is responsible for keeping air from getting in and out of your wine.

The airlock applies alongside a stopper that fits through the bottle's neck. The airlock keeps the stopper in the neck and ensures there is enough pressure applied. A #8 or #9 stopper should be good enough.

The airlock and stopper are available through most retailers for less than $10. Each part should be flexible enough to fit into the bottle and force itself into the neck to keep air from being a threat.

STIRRER

A stirrer is required for mixing the wine. A plastic handle is often good enough although a metal unit might work better. It does not have lots of pores in its body.

You should find a stirrer for just a few dollars. Get several stirrers on hand, so you won't use the same one too many times. You do not want to use the same one several times over as it might be hard to support after a while.

Some stirrers may be marketed as models designed for preparing fine cocktails. These might sound attractive and fancy but just make sure the stirrer you get is long enough for your containers. The stirrer should go well into your wine so it mixes everything up without your hands getting in direct contact with the wine.

FUNNEL

A funnel is to be added at the top of a bottle or carboy to pour liquid into that vessel. This keeps the liquid in the vessel without it spilling all around. You should not spend more than just a few dollars on a funnel.

The funnel does not have to be overly large. Just make the funnel large enough to where the siphon tube gets into the middle space. Do not waste too much space with getting it secured.

TURKEY BASTER

A basic turkey baster should be added for sampling purposes. With a turkey baster, you will gently take out some of your wine from the carboy for sampling. This is to be done after fermentation so you get a clear idea of how well your wine is being made.

This is another tool that only costs a few dollars. It is indispensable for when you are checking on the individual wine samples you are producing.

BOTTLES FOR THE FINAL PRODUCT

Two-liter bottles and jugs for wine are available through some retailers. These cost a few dollars each and feature dark tones to keep light from getting into your wine.

You have the option to take your old bottles from your home and use them for storage purposes. You would have to sterilize all your bottles to make them suitable for storage needs.

All of these items should be prepared properly for the wine-making process. Get everything you need as soon as possible so it will not be tough to prepare your wines.

CHAPTER 6 - GATHERING OR GROWING GRAPES

THE next part of getting wine ready is to get the grapes needed for it. Grapes are important for how they produce the juices needed for great wines.

Grapes are found in many forms, as you noticed earlier. Any kind of grape will do though. But when getting your grapes, you have to look at how well they are made. You have the option to buy grapes or to order grape vines that you could grow your grapes on.

The grapes you have must be ready for consumption. They should be fully ripe and ready for fermentation. Your grape must also be easy to press and crush. Review how well your grapes are prepared and you will find that it is not hard to get the most out of them.

BUYING GRAPES

It might be a challenge for you to grow grape vines. Fortunately, you do have the option to buy grapes from your local grocery store if desired. But you must look for organic grapes if possible.

The problem with finding grapes at supermarkets is that you never know if they are safe to use for your wine-making needs. Some of these grapes might be treated with chemical compounds. Too many farms these days use such compounds to make it easier for them to grow and survive against various diseases.

There are many organic grocery stores out there that offer grapes that have not been treated with chemicals:

- Local farmer's markets often have grapes that are made without any pesticides or other chemicals. See if any farmers who grow these grapes are on site while a market is open. Ask questions about the grapes and how they are made.

- Various major grocery store chains have begun to offer organic sections. Kroger, Harris Teeter and Publix have been expanding upon the number of organic products around. The selection of options available for your organic needs may vary based on where you go.

- Places that focus on organic and natural foods are popular too. Spots like Trader Joe's and Whole Foods have spread out around the entire country. Meanwhile, regional grocers like Pathmark in the Mid-Atlantic and Hannaford in the northeast have become popular for focusing primarily on organics.

Look for grapes that are truly organic. Do not stick with anything that was processed or modified in any way.

WHAT ABOUT THE SPECIFIC WINE GRAPES?

The grapes you would find at a local market are typically basic ones. Those fruits are designed to be consumed on their own or mixed with salads among other everyday entrees.

But where can you find the ones that are made specifically with certain types of wine in mind? What can you do to get your hands on the fancy wines that people engineer solely for wine-making purposes? You should not just ask for any ordinary grapes. You need ones that stand out and offer some appealing textures.

It is much easier to find those fancy wine grapes in places where they are commonly used in. You might have a better shot at finding them in California or

New Mexico among other places where wines are commonly grown in.

You have the option to buy wines that come from vineyards around the country. This is provided that you are in a place where you can legally get specific grapes out to for wine-making purposes. Remember, there are rules in some parts of the country with regards to where you can legally get grapes out from for the purpose of making your wine.

It has never been easier to buy grapes for wine-making than it is now. You could buy grapes online from one of various retailers.

TIPS FOR BUYING GRAPES

It is true that many live grapes can be sent out to your property as soon as possible. But when ordering such grapes, you must look at a few things in mind:

- Think about the specific type of grape plant you are getting. Are the grapes you are ordering appropriate for a certain type of wine or could they be suited for practically anything you want?

- See when the grape plant is being shipped out to you. Sometimes you might get the grape plant in a few days after you order it. In other cases you would have to wait until a specific time period when the farmer can get it harvested. The window of delivery would be massive at that point.

- Review the standards the grape farmer uses for getting a particular shipment ready. Sometimes the farmer might use properly insulated materials to keep the grapes from being too warm while preventing them from shifting around during the shipping process.

Your grapes must be ready for consumption while being safe to use. You need to see how well those grapes are made so whatever you have is easy to make and use.

BUYING VINES

You have the option to buy vines that allow you to grow grapes. Various vines are available from a variety of great wineries. These places offer vines that can be planted into your soil and then monitored regularly. This is to give you great grapes that will stick around for years to come. This is intriguing to see but it helps to look at how well these plants may work.

Vines are similar to what you would find at a much larger vineyard. These are made with tall bodies that stand out from the soil and produce various grapes. Think about these are miniature trees of sorts.

There are a few things to see when buying vines:

- Look at how well the grapes grow off of a vine plant. They should be rather full-bodied.

- See how long a vine will last for. With proper care and regular maintenance, you could get a vine to last for two to four years.

- See when someone will ship out your vine to you. A vineyard might have to wait until a certain time of the year to get your shipment out. This is to ensure that a proper base for your vine is ready. This is also so the wine can be harvested at only the best possible time.

- Check on whether your plant can grow in soil where you are. Some plants do better in spots where the soil is a little warmer.

MAINTAINING GRAPES AND VINES

After getting a vine, look at how well you will maintain your plants. Keep the temperature comfortable while nourishing your plants properly so they can last long enough.

There are several points you must follow as you maintain your grape plants and vines:

- Plant your vines in the spring. This is around the time when they can start growing grapes.

- Soak the roots for a few hours before planting them. Let the roots feel stimulated.

- Find a space with enough sun. Natural light is required for triggering the vine's natural ability to produce grapes.

- Review the soil you add your plant into. It needs to be properly circulated and aerated. It must offer enough drainage so the vines will not be at risk of flooding.

- Check on the temperatures in your area as you are growing your plants. The best conditions are in the spring when the weather is relatively cool even as the vines get enough sunlight for stimulation. Refer to the earlier section for details on the best weather conditions for individual grape plants.

- Review the fertilization standards needed for a plant. All grape plants have their needs for fertilizer or other growth compounds. Some might not require anything extra as they feature self-fertile bodies. The group that sells you a vine should give you information on how to use fertilizer and what needs to be in it (provided fertilizer is required in the process).

- Create a support beam like a trellis around your vine before you plant it. A grape vine must be trained to stand upright if it is young. This not only strengthens the plant but also prevents diseases from developing.

All these plans for growing a vine must be used carefully. You have to keep your plant steady and active if you want to get the most grapes out of it.

GATHERING THE GRAPES

You should be ready to get your grapes for the wine once they have become fully grown. After a while, the grapes should appear ripe and full-bodied in color and appearance.

The harvesting process should take place during the summer or fall season. The warmer temperatures of the summer allow for the grapes to grow and mature. The cooler temperatures are simply there to make it easier for the plants to germinate and produce new buds.

Sample a few grapes from your vines as needed. See that they taste well. Do not use them just yet if you cannot identify a flavor or if the grapes feel too rough.

You can store your grapes for up to six weeks at a time in a cellar. Keep them separate from other foods so nothing gets in the way of their textures.

You should start preparing your wine as soon as possible. The wine plants should be prepared well so the wine will taste its best in the end.

Regardless of whether you buy your grapes or plant them yourself, you should see that the grapes you get are suitable for your wine plans. Look for ones that are easy to work with and do not require too much stress on your part to make them ready for use.

CHAPTER 7 – STERILIZE YOUR EQUIPMENT

STERILIZATION is a practice that entails getting rid of bacteria off of any surface. Very sensitive materials are always sterilized to keep people from being at risk of getting in contact with harmful compounds.

When was the last time you went to a hospital? You might have noticed some of the extensive materials used by a hospital to clean off utensils. Sometimes you might see individual items that are wrapped for single use because they have been fully sterilized beforehand.

The general point is that sterilization is necessary for keeping items protected and at less of a risk of harming someone. This is a point that especially works for when you are trying to consume foods. Companies that make food products always sterilize their machines and utensils so anything they prepare is safe for consumption.

You must put in your own sterilization effort into the process of making wine. But to make this work, you have to use the proper materials for cleaning off items the right way.

Before you get started with making wine, you have to sterilize your equipment. On the surface, you might think that your equipment is clean. A clear surface and no visible traces of dirt might suggest everything is good to go.

But even the smallest things could be stuck inside your containers and other bits of equipment. Even the minutest forms of bacteria could get around your equipment.

Every piece of equipment you use should be sterilized. This means that every surface is cleaned down with all bits of bacteria killed off in the process.

I know, this does not sound like a very fun part of the process. But it is the most important part when it is all considered. The goal is to create a smooth and strong surface for wine-making.

A quick note: The sterilization process must work even if you have completely new materials for your wine-making plans. Just because something has never been used in the past does not mean it could have some bacteria. You never know what something might collect while in transit or storage.

START BY CLEANING

Before you sterilize your equipment, you have to clean each piece out. The basic cleaning process is done before the sterilization occurs. As you clean your surfaces, you get rid of old dirt and bacteria compounds. These include some of the more visible materials you might find around your utensils.

Any kind of soap may be utilized but do try and find something a little stronger if possible. Here are two of the more commonplace compounds you may use for cleaning off your equipment.

PERCARBONATES

Look for percarbonates for your cleaning needs. These contain hydrogen peroxide and sodium carbonate. These remove dirt and other deposits from all around.

Percarbonates use a mix of active oxygen and an alkali agent to lift off bacteria and dirt. Hydrogen peroxide offers a slight bit of cleansing.

These are ideal for cleaning off difficult stains. The use of oxygen especially does well for taking care of your surface. Do keep percarbonates from being stuck on your materials for too long though.

CHLORINE

Chlorine is traditionally used in swimming pools but it also fits in well for wine-making. Chlorine is a bleach-like compound that has been slightly diluted to where it is safe to process. That is, the substance is not as toxic as straightforward bleach.

Add around two and a half tablespoons of chlorine for every five gallons of water. Let this soak for around 30 minutes. Rinse off the chlorine and water mix with clean water so any residues that might be stuck are properly removed.

Chlorine works best if you have glass materials. It will not work on plastic or stainless steel surfaces. Chlorine could break through those materials.

Watch for how well the chlorine is washed off too. See that any streaks produced are cleared off properly. Any streaks that persist might be signs of chlorine deposits that are still stuck on a surface. Wash off those materials as soon as possible so everything is treated right.

Sanitization Plans

The sanitization process focuses heavily on ensuring that all compounds are sealed and secured without outside problems getting in the way. To sanitize a surface, add one of the following options with water. The solution you produce should soak for about five to ten minutes on average and then be rinsed off with clean water. Some solutions require you to rinse them off sooner.

Chlorine

While chlorine does indeed help with the cleansing process, it also works as a sanitizer. You would have to add a quarter of a teaspoon of chlorine with each gallon of water. Allow it to soak for a few minutes and then rinse it off.

You could always add chlorine to your wine-making items even if you already used chlorine to clean them off a few minutes earlier. The first chlorine application must be fully washed off before the second one can be added.

IODINE

Iodine is another attractive sanitizing agent for your use. Add 2 to 4 mL of iodine for every gallon of water. Do not let this stick around for too long though. Iodine is poisonous if kept around for a while or if you add too much. Rinse off the iodine with clean water after a minute.

CAMPDEN TABLETS WITH POTASSIUM

Campden tablets have been used in the wine-making industry for generations. Such tablets contain potassium metabisulfite. This inhibits the production of bacteria.

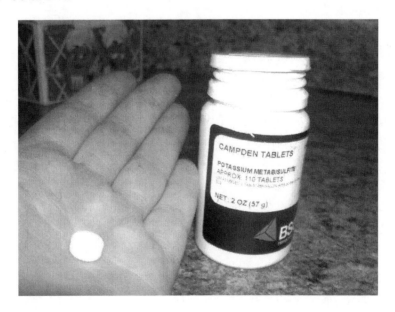

Such tablets are properly measured to fit into most wine-making vessels.

A single tablet typically features 67 mg of potassium metabisulfite for every liter per gallon. You do not even require any water for rinsing.

These tablets are available in packets through many wine-making resource websites. Such items are tried and true for being easy to use and mix. In fact, you could get one of these tablets added into your carboy after you open it up following weeks of fermentation. The process keeps bacteria from getting into the wine right away. You will learn a little more about that later in another chapter.

B-BRITE

B-Brite is a powder compound designed with wine-making functions in mind. It works alongside active oxygen to clean off surfaces. It has no chlorine or bisulfites. This even removes old residues from prior fermentation processes.

Only one tablespoon of B-Brite is needed for every gallon of water used. Rinse the material off after soaking it for about five to ten minutes.

The general point about these sanitizing agents is that they are all easy to apply and will clean off numerous surfaces. Look at each option and figure out the one that you know works best for your plans. This includes something easy to wash off and apply without problems.

In summary, here are a few standards to follow for each of these sanitizing items:

Sanitizing Agent	Mixing Rules	Benefits	Concerns
Chlorine	¼ teaspoon for every gallon of water for about 5 to 15 minutes	Easy to find	Tough to remove from porous surfaces
Iodine	2 to 4 mL for every gallon of water for 60 seconds	Simple and easy to use	Do not use too much; it is toxic in high quantities
Campden Tablets with Potassium	Crush 14 tablets and dissolve them in about a gallon of water	Last for a while and do not require any additional rinsing	Contains some sulfites
B-Brite	Add one tablespoon for every	Works with oxygen; it may also	A little more

	gallon of water and soak for 5 to 10 minutes	work as a cleanser in addition to being a sanitizer	expensive to find

CAN SODIUM-BASED CAMPDEN TABLETS WORK?

Campden tablets that contain sodium can be found in some places but it is becoming harder to get them these days. This comes as these tablets might be risky. The sodium inside these tablets makes it harder for you to make it work right.

These contain sodium metabisulfite, a compound that has long been used in the cleaning process for generations. Winemakers all around the world have used these tablets to clear out stubborn deposits within vats and other surfaces.

Such tablets are not as common as there are concerns over how these tablets might cause the flavors in wines to change. Also, there are worries about adding more sodium into wine. The quality of wine might be compromised slightly when sodium is added. As a result, it is nowhere near as easy for you to find sodium-based Campden tablets today as it was in the past.

You are better off using potassium-based tablets instead. These tablets are easier to prepare and use without problems.

CAN'T YOU JUST BOIL THE MATERIALS?

You always have the option to simply boil your wine-making materials if you prefer. Boiling is always worthwhile as it produces heat through water to kill off various surfaces. No chemicals are needed in the process.

As you boil something, the water that you wash things in becomes fully cleaned off. More importantly, it becomes harder for bacteria to survive. As the bacteria is burned off, the surfaces become cleaner and safer.

You would have to boil your materials in water that is at least 170 degrees Fahrenheit for around five to ten minutes.

You would require plenty of heat and a large vessel for you to wash your materials off in. Be cautious when boiling as well as the process can be very risky if not controlled well enough.

Also, any materials you use for drying off a surface must be checked well. All drying agents must be clean and safe to use. While you could use a towel to dry off a surface, it needs to be soft and fully clean.

If anything, using warm air to dry off a surface might be your best bit. This is just to keep it from getting in contact with any outside surfaces that might actually be harmful.

All of these options for taking care of the sterilization process should make a real difference. You must look at how strong the process works so everything you use for making wine will be clean.

CHAPTER 8 - USING YOUR GRAPES

THE efforts you put into getting your grapes ready to be made into wine should be taken just as seriously as the efforts used for acquiring them. Originally, I thought all you had to do was just crush the grapes and place them in a reservoir. But as it turns out, there are lots of things that have to be done to ensure that grapes are treated right.

You must prepare your grapes correctly so they are ready for use. Look at how well you can get them ready so the juices from those grapes work to your benefit.

CLEAN OFF THE GRAPES

Now it is time to look at how well you can prepare your grapes. You have to look at how well the grapes are made so they are suitable for wine-making.

To make it all work, start by cleaning off your grapes. This is a necessity for getting the natural flavors of the grapes out:

1. Remove the stems and leaves.

2. Look for bits of dirt on the grapes. Get as many of those bits scraped off as possible without damaging the grapes.

3. Add the grapes into a clean colander or other drainer.

4. Use cool water to rinse them off. Use filtered water as tap water might contain additives that influence the taste of your wine.

5. Place the grapes into a proper crock or other vessel.

You do have the option to peel off the skins from your grapes if desired. This would produce a lighter wine if you do this. Keeping the skins on creates a deeper flavor. Of course, it also produces the detailed red tone that you might expect out of some wines.

Also, some winemakers like to prepare their wines without washing them off. They do this with the belief that the unwashed skins can produce yeast when they are in contact with air during the fermentation process.

For our example, I would recommend you wash off the grapes anyway. It is best to use a safe process for your first time with preparing wine.

CRUSHING THE GRAPES

After washing off your grapes (and peeling off their skins if you wish), you must crush them. You could use your hands to do this although a cleaned-off masher might be good enough.

As you crush the grapes, you will release their natural juices.

Here are some specific steps for the crushing process:

1. Use a firm masher to crush your grapes.

2. Keep crushing them until the fruit juice level inside your contain is within one and a half inches of the top of your container. Filtered water may be utilized to get you closer to the top if necessary.

3. Add a potassium-based Campden tablet to kill off any wild bacteria or yeast. This step is completely optional but it might help to preserve the quality of the grapes. You also

have the option to add two cups of boiling water over the grapes to kill off the bacteria.

These steps should provide you with a good base to start with. But after that, you need to get a bit of yeast added into the mix. The next chapter focuses on what you can do with yeast.

This masher is a good example of what you could find for taking care of your grapes. Anything that crushes your grapes well and offers enough coverage is worthwhile.

(If you are making large quantity or for business, use this type of masher)

The interesting thing about mashing grapes is that people have used all sorts of processes for doing so over the years. Some people crushed their grapes by foot in the past. Others would use hammers or just massive weights. Today wine-making has evolved to where you just need a good masher material to cut your grapes down.

A QUICK NOTE ON FRUIT JUICES

Some people like to use fruit juices for their wines. People often use grape juice instead of actual grapes when trying to make wines.

I get that this is an appealing and quick solution for making wine. But I would not recommend using a fruit juice in lieu of actual grapes.

The problem with so many grape juices is that they are augmented with excess sugars and compounds. These include additives that go beyond ascorbic acid or vitamin C, the only compound that your grapes should have.

These additions often come about regardless of the type of juice you order. Just because one company says that it offers 100-percent pure grape juice doesn't mean it consists of nothing but the juices that come out of grapes. Some additives might have been included in the mix just to preserve the grape juice or to add a bit of flavor to it. Such items would only compromise the quality of the wine you would try to produce.

Many fruit juices are packaged in a series of plastic bottles. The plastic compounds in those bottles might be an issue. They could shed off and get into your juice over time. This only keeps the juice from being pure.

Also, the added sugars that come with grape juices could overwhelm the final product. A greater amount of sugar produces a higher amount of alcoholic content within your wine, thus making it dangerous. Sticking with the natural sugars that come with actual grapes is always worthwhile.

I am not saying that you should avoid using grape juices or other fruit juices. You have the right to use these when trying to make wine for the first time. Just don't expect the results to be anywhere near as great as what you would get out of actual grapes in the wine-making process.

CHAPTER 9 - WORKING WITH YEAST

YEAST is a necessity for getting your wine to grow. Yeast is applied into the wine to help bolster the fermentation process.

Yeast is by far the most critical ingredient to add into the wine-making process. Yeast converts the sugars in your wine into alcohol and carbon dioxide. This works as oxygen is harder to come across while preparing your wine.

The fermentation process should be reviewed properly. The wine must be secured in a sealed area with yeast added to ensure the alcoholic content is produced.

You can find yeast in many places including your local supermarket. Baker's yeast works well enough for your wine-making demands.

HOW MUCH IS NEEDED?

The good news is that yeast for wine-making is typically sold in packets. A single packet may be good enough for one to five gallons of wine.

Feel free to use the entire singular yeast packet for your wine provided it is within the range of coverage listed on its body.

The fermentation process will probably go a little faster if you have a smaller amount of wine to work with. This should be useful but at the same time you have to be cautious. You must test the wine regularly to see that it is responding well to the yeast.

ADDING THE YEAST

The process of adding the yeast into the wine should be rather simple. Just add the yeast into the crushed grapes and then use a long-handled spoon. Stick with a fully sanitized spoon.

Watch as the yeast and grapes create a slight foamy surface. This surface is known as a must.

A QUICK TIP: USE HONEY

One good idea to use is to add honey while you apply yeast. Honey is ideal for how it supports the yeast. It becomes easier for the yeast to develop and spread around the wine.

Although this is indeed an appealing option for making the yeast work, you must be careful when adding honey. The amount of honey you add could influence the overall flavor of your wine. Honey might make the wine a little sweeter.

It is completely optional for you to add honey into your wine. This is great for managing yeast but it is not always required.

You could add about a cup of honey into the mixture if desired. That total should provide your yeast with enough support for developing and growing.

Do watch for the particular flavor you want to establish out of your wine though. Be certain when getting your wine ready that you are careful with it and that you understand what you want to make out of it in general.

CHAPTER 10 – GETTING THE EQUIPMENT READY

AFTER you have gotten the grapes and yeast prepared, you need to get the equipment for the rest of the process ready. This is to ensure the fermentation process can start well.

KEEP EVERYTHING STERILIZED

I already discussed how the sterilization process works in an earlier shaper in this guide. Refer back to that chapter if necessary. I cannot emphasize it enough though – sterilization is critical so your wine will ferment in a spot where outside materials will not influence your win.

CHECK THE BODY OF THE EQUIPMENT

In addition to your equipment being fully sterilized, you have to check on how the bodies of each piece you use are made. See that your storage vessels contain no cracks, chips or other imperfections. You have to keep them cleaned off are ready for use.

A good idea would be to look at the tinting on your glass. While clear glass is often useful, it helps to keep clear glass in a spot where there isn't much light in a spot. You do not want excess light to get in the way of your wine and cause it to weaken.

Don't worry if you cannot find anything with a tint on it though. Tinting is optional but still recommended with regards to keeping light from being an issue. Then again, storing the glass in a dark space is always the right thing to do just to keep it safe and secure from outside issues.

Anything that does not fully close up or support your individual bits of equipment should be discarded. Be ready to trash anything that might be tough to use or incapable of giving you a comfortable space for preparing wine.

GET A PROPER LID

A lid should be added over the large container used for fermenting your win. The huge container needs something that keeps bugs and other outside items from getting into the wine but still allow for a bit of air to move through.

Look for a crock lid that offers for a slight bit of air to move through. This should be enough to offer a comfortable space for the wine to be made ready in.

The lid must also offer a secure fit that does not slip off easily. The lid has to be strong and sturdy enough but still easy to support.

Now that you have all the materials on hand, you can start with the fermentation process. The wine that you produced should be ready to get into proper containers.

CHAPTER 11 – THE FERMENTATION PROCESS

THE fermentation process must be followed carefully. It takes a few days and requires effort on your part to monitor the wine and stir it regularly. You must especially watch for the bubbling motion that comes along when the yeast gets in full control with the grapes. Here are some steps to use to get the most out of it.

COVER THE MAIN JAR

After the wine grapes have been crushed and yeast has been added, stir everything and then secure a cover over the main jar. Keep the cover tight and sealed but make sure a small opening can be found on one part of the jar just to allow air to move through.

Keep the jar in a spot set at around 70 degrees Fahrenheit overnight. Keep the area slightly warm so the yeast will grow. Do not keep it too hot or else the yeast will die off.

STIR REGULARLY

Stir the wine frequently as the fermentation starts. Do this one every four hours at the start. Following that, stir the mixture a few times more every day for the next three to four days.

Notice the bubbling motion in the wine. The yeast is working at this point. It is converting the sugar into alcohol.

Keep your stirrer cleaned off after each use. Having multiple stirrers always helps.

STRAINING THE WINE

Move the wine from your larger jar to the carboy for storage after the bubbling dies down. It takes about three to five days for the bubbling to stop.

At this point, the wine should be kept in secure storage. It keeps to be sealed off so the gases produced by the yeast interacting with the grapes produce the alcohol content and detailed flavors you would expect to get out of your wine.

Take your tubing and siphon the wine out from the jar to the carboy. Refer to the instructions listed a few chapters ago on how a siphoning tube works.

Look at how well the wine is being strained at this point. The tube should be narrow enough to take in the wine while leaving any old wine skins or other pulp materials behind. You could also use a strainer at the very top end of the carboy to keep some of the pulp materials out.

Use the funnel to secure the wine into the carboy so it does not spill off onto the side.

After that, apply the airlock and stopper onto the carboy. This should create a secure barrier where air will not get into the bottle.

HOW LONG SHOULD IT REST FOR?

Allow the wine to age for a while. Although you could enjoy your wine about a month after you make it, you might be better off waiting a few extra months. Give it around six months if possible. That should be enough to allow the flavor to mature.

Add a few extra months if you used honey like what was mentioned earlier. Your wine might be too sweet if the honey has not aged.

Be free to let your wine rest for as long as you want but do let it age well enough to at least improve upon the taste of your wine. Look at how well you can get your wine ready so you do not struggle with anything unusual.

PREPARING A GOOD TEMPERATURE

The most important thing for fermenting your wine is ensuring it is kept at a consistent temperature. Do not allow the temperature to keep going up or down. Instead, give yourself time to let the temperature stay secure and consistent.

Keep the temperature at around 68 to 78 degrees Fahrenheit as you ferment the wine. It takes less time for the wine to ferment when you use this standard.

There are a few things you can use when getting the temperature set up properly:

- A brewing or heating belt could be applied around your wine storage tank. This is an electric cable that goes around the container and offers a slight amount of heat.

- A heat tray could go under the fermentation space. The flat tray adds plenty of heat although you'd have to watch for how much wine such a tray can handle at a given time. A heat tray may handle up to five gallons of wine at a time.

- An immersion heater goes into a heater and directly gets in contact with the wine. This is similar to what you'd see in a fish tank. It adds direct heat but it is not always recommended due to some of the added compounds that might be around the body of the heater.

This plan for fermenting your wine takes a while but it is critical for giving you the best flavor possible.

MONITORING THE WINE

Keep tabs on your wine as it matures. Check on how the wine looks inside its carboy as it ferments. See that the wine's color looks consistent.

Stir the wine if you see any bubbling motions. This might be a sign of some bits of yeast getting late into the game.

Use a turkey baster after a few weeks or months to get a quick taste of the wine. A small amount is enough to give you an idea of whether it is ready for consumption or if you need it to mature a little longer.

No matter what happens, be sure you look at how well the wine tastes and that it is developing properly. Check around to see how well it looks.

CHAPTER 12 - STORING YOUR WINE

AFTER you have finished fermenting your wine, you can get it stored. But you must watch for how the wine is secured so it doesn't age prematurely or wear out.

Your wine is especially vulnerable right as you open it up. Keeping it secured with the right protective measures makes a real difference.

ADD A CAMPDEN TABLET

Keep the wine secure after you open up your carboy. Add a Campden tablet into the wine and allow it to dissolve. The tablet keeps the wine from reacting with any bacteria that might come about after the carboy opens.

You must use this tablet so the wine will not become vinegar. Your wine is very vulnerable as you get the carboy opened up. Using a tablet keeps the wine safe.

GET THE SIPHONING TUBE READY

Next, gather the siphoning tube again and move the wine from the carboy into your bottles. Do this with as many bottles as you have.

Fill each bottle to the near top and then use a cork to secure each one immediately. Keep a firm plug on each bottle with your corks. Allow them to move deep into each bottle.

For the best results, use dark-colored wine bottles. These keep the wines from oxidation issues related to light exposure. Dark bottles do well for red wines as they preserve the wine's natural color.

ALLOW THE WINE TO AGE

Give your wine a bit of extra time to age. While the fermentation process should have done well for getting the yeast to mix perfectly with the wine, you should still give it an extra bit. Allow the wine to stay inside a bottle and let it relax for a bit. Give some time for the wine to age and stay strong.

HOW WARM CAN A STORAGE AREA BE?

Keep the wine stored in a climate-controlled area as well. Keeping your wine at room temperature helps but there are a few points to look into when getting such a storage area arranged:

- Wines can typically handle conditions of up to 70 degrees Fahrenheit without suffering serious problems.

- A wine chiller is ideal for storage. Keep your wines at conditions from 52 to 60 degrees inside such a small cooler.

- Keep your wine bottles stored on their sides. That is, place a bottle on its side instead of upright. The wine stays moist at this point. Also, the wine is smoother when stored this way. Racks or coolers should have surfaces that let you store your bottles on their sides.

- Avoid putting your bottles out in the light even if they are tan or dark in color. The risk of light causing your wines to age quickly is a real problem.

By using these steps, it becomes easy for you to get more out of your wine. Be careful when storing your wine so you have an extra bit of control over how it works and what you are getting off of it.

So, now you know how to prepare wine in your home and how to store it properly. Let's look at a few more points relating to wine, particularly what you could do to make money off of your newfound skill.

CHAPTER 13 - WHAT ABOUT OTHER FRUITS?

YOU have read all about making wines through grapes in this guide. It is only sensible that we focus on grapes as those are the things that make wine distinct. But did you know that you could also make wines with fruits?

Fruit wine is a form of wine that is made from a fruit other than the grape. This form of wine has been popular in many parts of the world, particularly in Asia where plum wine is commonly found in.

WHAT FRUITS WORK?

You could get juices from one of various fruits ready. Cherries, apples, plums, oranges and pineapples are among the most popular fruits that you could use.

But no matter what you choose, you must look at how well you add yeast into the fruit wine. You must measure the yeast carefully so only the right amount can be added into the wine, thus allowing it to ferment properly.

Also, any pits, seeds or other items inside the fruit must be removed. Some pits and cores in various fruits might be dangerous. They will typically not produce any added flavors either.

You do have the option to keep the peels and skins inside your wine reservoir during the fermentation process. This could add an extra bit of flavor into your fruit.

TIPS FOR WORKING WITH FRUITS

As you utilize fruits, it helps to look for a few points. Many of these relate to specific fruits you could apply into your wine:

- Raisins often add a bit of sweetness to your wine. The body of the wine may be a little bolder too.

- Bananas add an extra bit of body to your wine.

- You still have the option to add grapes to your fruit wine. Grape concentrate is best though as it adds a bit of extra character without overwhelming the fruity tones of the wine you are making.

- Adding sugar to your fruit wine also keeps it preserved.

- Organic fruits are clearly better for how they are healthy and safe to consume. They do not have any potentially harmful chemicals and should have their natural flavors fully intact without any threats added.

The process for making fruit wine should be identical to the process used for making more traditional wines with grapes in them. Look around to see what can work though. Be willing to experiment with different kinds of wines if you wish.

PART 2

STARTING YOUR WINE MAKING BUSINESS

CHAPTER 14 - HOW TO SELL YOUR WINE

CURRENTLY, laws around the United States say that you can only provide your homemade wine to people without charging anything and that you cannot just give it away to the public. But did you know that you can sell wine without getting into trouble if you put in enough effort into it?

The process involved for selling your wine to the public will require you to go through a few legal points. But once you get through them all, it becomes easy for you to sell your wine.

Note: All points listed here are for United States residents only. Check with your local alcohol control bureau or government office to learn about what can be done in your country with regards to selling wine.

CHECK THE TTB

The Alcohol and Tobacco Tax and Trade Bureau is an operation of the United States Department of the Treasury. This group provides licenses and approvals to those looking to make wines.

You must file an application with the TTB if you want to sell wine for commercial purposes. Your entity qualifies as a bonded winery when registered with the TTB.

But the TTB does require you to fill out numerous forms. These are produced by the TTB National Revenue Center and entail applications for establishing a wine business, getting a wine bond and listing information on environmental and water quality standards where you are. Such documents identify the legal nature of your work, what you are doing and where it is taking place. Points on the safety of the grapes and other items inside your locality must be added as well.

Visit https://www.ttb.gov/wine/federal_app.shtml to learn more about the applications you would have to fill out. Read all the instructions carefully as it entails not only what you have to include but also points on taxes and other charges involved.

Now let's focus more on why and how to get a wine business started.

CHAPTER 15 - 4 REASONS YOU SHOULD START A WINE MAKING BUSINESS

TO me, Wine making is a great at home business. There are so many varities of wines, and the types of wines you can make are only limited by your imagination. Consider the following reasons why you should start a wine making business of your own.

THE HIGH DEMAND FOR WINES

Since wines have so many varieties, you are getting into a market that has high demand. When there is a high demand for a product, it is easier to make your business successful. The sales of wines particularly increase during festive times such as Easter, Valentine's Day, Thanksgiving, and Christmas.

WINE MAKING ISN'T CAPITAL INTENSIVE

There is little investment to start a wine making business. The cost to make wines is also low with a healthy profit margin. This makes it favorable to start a wine making business.

WINE MAKING ISN'T LABOR INTENSIVE

To get started with wine making you don't need to have a huge business with ten employees. You can make few bottles of wines a day on your own without needing any extra help. Again this makes it easy to start your business, and you only have to expand when you're ready and have the money to do so. Remember you don't need to make 100 or 1000 bottles a day to have a business, start slow, maybe supply to just one or two local wine shops at first and see how the customers respond to your creation.

A VERSATILE BUSINESS

Perhaps the best aspect of starting a wine making business is that it can be very versatile. There is little investment needed, and you can choose to make anything from simple to elaborate wines; while still finding a great market.

CHAPTER 16 - 6 ESSENTIAL ASPECTS OF WINE MAKING BUSINESS

NOW that we know why to start a wine making business let's look at what you need to do to start your own wine making business. There are some essential aspects you need to know about starting a wine making business.

LEARN YOUR MARKET DEMAND BY MINI MARKET RESEARCH

There are two things you need to know about the wines you plan to make. First, you want to know what type of wines you are interested in making. Second, you want to know what kind of wines you'll be able to sell to target customers.

In other words, it is best to find out what your customers want rather than telling or offering them what you think they want. If you spend a little time talking to local people and ask them what they like in wines, you may be surprised at what you find out. This is what I call mini market research.

A lot of people make the mistake of making a certain type of wines that they like thinking everyone else would love them too, but in reality, you may have a very different taste or choice than the mainstream folks, so it is best to do the market research and find out what people really like.

Most wine makers enjoy working with this hobby because it is something they like to do. You will get your most pleasure out of working with what you enjoy: the type of grapes you work with, the colors you choose, the fragrances you prefer and the flavors you find attractive. Your personal preferences matter a lot when it comes to making wines and doing a hobby you enjoy. It is important to enjoy what you are going to do if you are going to make it a full-time business.

However, this might be different when it comes to your target market. Different people, looking for different things are going to buy different wines. For example, some food fairs can be a great way to sell wines. Although you may do better selling simple wines rather than fine wines at these fairs. So like I just said earlier it is important to do market research when starting your wine making business to make sure you are not only making what you enjoy but also making a wine that is going to make your business profitable.

KNOW THE PROCESS

To be successful in the wine making business, you need to have a great product. The wines you make need to make your customers happy. Even if you are making simple table wines for everyday consumtion, they should still taste great and be priced appropriately.

If you are going to sell fine aged wines, you want to be well practiced at making them aged properly so the flavor is not lost. The more you know and learn about making wines, the better your products will be. The better your wines, the more profitable your business becomes. One word of advice I want to offer here, try not to make or market wines that will retail for over $20, at first try making something simple with a price point that is under $20 per bottle.

When you are well versed in the wine making process, you will also be better able to experiment with different packaging, colors, and bottle sizes so you can increase your range of products.

Learning as much as you can about wine making also allows you to make wines efficiently with as little wastage as possible. This is important to your business's bottom line and keeps the cost of your business low. This means an increased profit margin for each wine bottle you sell. So take the time to learn as much as you can about wine making.

THE BUSINESS ASPECT

When starting a business, no matter how small, there are a number of rules and regulations you need to follow. Since wine is alcohol, it comes it some extra regulations and requirements, so doing your research for your own city, state and country would be an important first step. It is important you research what rules there are for small business start-ups in your local area. Then make sure you follow these rules. It is important to have a legal and official business entity if you are looking to grow your business into a larger business eventually.

When starting your own business, you also want to give careful consideration to things such as branding, packaging and the business plan. Doing all of this will ensure your business becomes a success.

Some of these don't need to be done at the beginning, but you should definitely start with a business plan. This will help you outline that steps that need to be followed. Your business plan will tell you when you need to create a brand and when is the best time to start an online store. The business plan is the roadmap for a small business.

It will keep you going and make sure you don't miss any important steps and avoid any mistakes. The business plan doesn't need to be anything elaborate; just a few pages can be sufficient. You can visit Bplans.com as they are one of the top companies to provide customize business plans.

Remember, to create a brand, a logo, and a beautiful packaging design do not cost as much as they used to, how may you ask? Well, there are many online talent sites where you can hire talented graphic designers for very little money and have them create some awesome logo, brand and packaging designs for you that are trendy, attractive and easy to produce.

I hired my graphic designer for 99dessign.com, and I believe I paid $250 for all three designs. But if you are on a tighter budget, try Fiverr.com, here you can find and hire designers for $5 to do each task. You will be amazed at how talented some of these designers truly are.

At this site, you can find talents that can help you with your social media and other marketing needs too; you can find talent that will do your flyer design to business cards all for $5 each. I am finding different ways to use Fiverr every day.

KNOW YOUR TARGET MARKET

Before you start your business, you also want to make sure you know where and how you're going to sell your wines. Determine who your customers are going to before you start to make your wines. The market research I just spoke about can also tell you who your potential customers will be.

Just make a note of every group and every venue you think you can sell your wines to. Then approach them with samples, flyers, or even just your business cards and introduce yourself.

FINDING THE BEST WHOLESALER TO SOURCE YOUR SUPPLIES

You should also consider your supply sources. This will have a direct impact on the cost of your wines and the bottom-line profit margin of your business. Depending on where you live, you may have a few local wholesalers that are offering good pricing on grapes and other raw material. One advice here, if you can source your grapes locally instead of online, do it since grapes are perishable and tend to be heavy when buying in bulk, it will save you a lot of money in shipping expenses.

As for most of the other nonperishable supplies, try to find a couple of reputable online retailers and always cross check prices and quality between them before buying. I don't buy from one or two online wholesalers, but I buy from many. This way I am always cross checking who has the best price and quality as they tend to vary widely.

DEVELOP BUSINESS SKILLS

As a small business owner you are going to have to wear a few hats. Therefore it is important that you learn business skills such as accounting, budgeting, design, etc.

Let's take a look at a general timeline for what you need to do to start your wine making business.

CHAPTER 17 - TIMELINE FOR STARTING A WINE MAKING BUSINESS

1. Learn how to making wines through a class or by reading about making wines.

2. Determine/identify a niche market for your business.

3. Develop a business plan to guide your business.

4. Obtain the necessary documentation required in your city/county/State to start a business.

5. Find which venues you want to use to sell your wines (Your target market).

6. Buy wholesale wine making supplies.

7. Join a wine makers association or a mastermind group.

8. Promote your wine making business through various promotions and marketing campaigns

Now that we've discussed the basics I want to go a little more in-depth. From my own experience, I've learned four important things you should do when starting a wine making business and five mistakes you need to avoid.

So let's take a look at what I learned, so you know what to do and what not to do.

CHAPTER 18 - 4 MUST DO'S

A S I've said, getting started with a wine making business is easy and doesn't require much. However, I've learned from experience and from talking to others in the industry that there are four specific things you need to do to get your business off to a good start.

NAME YOUR BUSINESS

You need to get customers to distinguish your product from others in the same industry. This means you are going to need a business name; and not just any name. You want a short name that is easy to remember while also being catchy.

You need to make sure the name you choose isn't being used by any other company. If you want to know about business names you need to contact the Patent and Trade Mark Office.

One good way to search is by searching the name you picked on Google to see if anyone else is using it for the same purpose. My advice is if you find a good name, go ahead and buy the domain name of the name you just picked, this way in future if you ever want to grow, you can have a website under that name.

You can go to Godaddy.com or name.com or any other domain name seller's site and just type the name you picked; they will tell you if that name is available for purchase with.com or .net. Typically most domain names cost around $10/year which in my opinion is a great investment.

LICENSE YOUR BUSINESS

All businesses need proper licenses to operate. This shows that you are running a legal business. However, before you are allowed to license a business, you need to determine a structure for your business. If you know an accountant or an attorney, ask them to file a legal business entity (Like an LLC, S Corp or LLP) on your behalf, this way you are legally protected from most business liabilities.

You can also go on websites like leaglzoom.com and have them draw up the document for less than what an attorney would charge you to do the same.

Once you file you file the article to incorporate your business, next step is to get an accountant or CPA to file and obtain an EIN(Employer's Identification Number) from IRS. This is similar to social security number but for business. Once you have these two documents, you can then open a commercial bank account at any local bank. I will touch more on various business entities and how to open a bank account in the next chapter.

Next step would be to go to your local city office and find out what type of business and regulatory licenses you are required to have. It should take a day or two to get your licenses and permits in place, and then you are finally and officially in business.

Once you have a business license and a trademark name, customers will trust your products and be more likely to buy them.

COMPETITIVE ANALYSIS

This is key to having a successful business. When you have a competitive analysis, you know your business's current position within the wine making industry.

The competitive analysis allows you to get the information you need on your competitors, market share, market strategies, growth and other important factors. When you have all this information, you will be able to change or improve your business in key areas so you can increase profits and sales.

Here is a simple way you can do a competitive analysis. On a piece of paper write down the following:

1. Number of local competitors you have
2. What is their niche/what type of wines they sell
3. Where they sell
4. What is their pricing

Once you have that list, take a look and see where you would fit in that list, how can you stand out from the crowd, what can you do differently that would make customers pay attention to your products.

In my business experience, I believe there are three ways you can always stand above the crowd. I always have tried to stand above the crowd by trying of these three strategies.

1. By making superior products than my competitors make
2. By offering 100% customer satisfaction guarantee
3. By creative pricing strategy

Let me explain what I mean by creative pricing strategy.

CREATIVE PRICING STRATEGY

Pricing is the most important factor of your business. A carefully thought out pricing strategy can make you very successful but a pricing strategy that places you above your market can literality put you out of business and on the other hand pricing below the market can wipe your bottom line profit completely clean, and before you know it, you are out of business and in debt.

That was the risky part; now the tricky part is if you stay with the market, then you are standing out in the crowd instead you are standing in the crowd. To make yourself more visible and unique and to stand tall among other competitors, you have to be really very creative when it comes to your pricing strategy, and that is where the tricky part comes is. My goal is to teach you how to implement a carefully thought out pricing strategy that can make you stand out and make you successful.

Here are few ideas I often try

1. Always run one special where you offer discount on one particular type of wine each month, but never the same type of wines every month

2. Run BOGO (Buy One Get One Free) promotion every few months on select wines (usually the ones that are not selling fast)

3. Never try to be the low price leader (It is a slippery slope, don't try to reduce your price just to stay competitive)

4. Run various package promotion during holidays (I usually make baskets with few wines, one bottle of aromatherapy essential oil, one soap and a wine holder all nicely wrapped)

Remember, when it comes to pricing or marketing ideas, there is no "one size fits all," not every idea works for everyone. Some strategies may work better for you than others and vice versa. So, it is a good idea to test each idea separately and document the results then analyze and see which one worked the best.

CHAPTER 19 - UNDERSTANDING PENNY PROFIT, PROFIT MARGIN, AND MARKUP

$\mathbf{I}$N business these are the three most common terms we hear every day, but what do they all mean and how they are different from each other, is a question many of you have. I know this because I get email time to time about this very topic.

Okay let's break them down and see what they are:

PENNY PROFIT

Penny profit is essentially the actual cash profit you make by selling any items in your store. For example, say you just sold a bottle of 20 oz. Coke $1.75, what is the penny profit of that sale? To find the answer first, we need to see how much you paid to buy that bottle of Coke. Looking at your invoice from Coke shows you paid $1.00 for that bottle of coke and you sold it for $1.75. So your penny profit is $1.75-1.00 = 75 cents. Penny profit is the difference between the selling price- actual costs.

PROFIT MARGIN

Profit margin the term most widely used and understood in most every business as it is what we all use to figure out if we are making enough profit from our businesses by selling the products and services.

Profit margin is essentially the percentage of profit you make or earn when you sell a product. Confusing? Let's take a look at the same example of that bottle of coke we just used earlier.

We already know the penny profit from that sale was 75 cents. Now the profit margin is done little differently, to find out the exact margin we will have to take the penny profit and divide that number by the selling price. So it will be $1.75-$1.00=0.75, then we divide that penny profit by the selling price 0.75/$1.75 = 43% profit margin.

MARKUP

The markup, on the other hand, is somewhat similar to profit margin, but instead of dividing the penny profit by the selling price you would have to divide the penny profit by the actual cost. Let's take a look at the same example once again.

Remember our penny profit from that bottle ok Coke? It was 75 cents; now we just need to divide that by the actual cost which was a $1.00 right? Let's do this, 0.75/$1.00 = 75% Markup for that same bottle of Coke.

CHAPTER 20 - DEALING WITH THE LEGALITY OF YOUR BUSINESS

INCORPORATING YOUR BUSINESS

When you choose a legal entity for your wine business there are two main factors to consider:

1. What you want

2. The type of business model you intend to build

Often you have the option of choosing to file as a limited liability company or LLC, general partnership or even sole proprietorship. A sole proprietorship is the ideal business structure for someone starting a wine making business, especially if it is a moderate start from you home. However, most prefer the benefits of an LLC.

If you plan to eventually expand your wine business to other locations or potentially online, then you definitely don't want to file as a sole proprietor. In this instance, you should definitely file as an LLC.

When you file as an LLC, you will be able to protect yourself from personal liability. This means that if anything goes wrong while operating your business then only the money you invested into the company is at risk. This isn't the case if you file as a sole proprietor or a general partnership. LLCs are simple and flexible to operate since you won't need a board of directors, shareholder meetings or other managerial formalities in order to run your business.

Here are all the legal business structures you can choose from, it is best to get some advice from your CPA or accountant or an attorney.

BUSINESS STRUCTURE

When starting a business, there are five different business structures you can choose from:

✧ Sole Proprietor

✧ Partnership

✧ Corporation (Inc. or Ltd.)

✧ S Corporation

✧ Limited Liability Company (LLC)

SOLE PROPRIETOR

This is not the safest structure for strarting a wine making business. It is used for a business owned by a single person or a married couple. Under this structure, the owner is personally liable for all business debts and may file on their personal income tax.

PARTNERSHIP

This is another inexpensive business structure to form. It often requires an agreement between two or more individuals who are going to jointly own and operate a business.

The partners will share all aspects of the business in accordance with the agreement. Partnerships don't pay taxes, but they need to file an informational return. Individual partners then report their share of profits and losses on their personal tax returns.

CORPORATION (INC. OR LTD.)

This is one of the more complex business structures and has the most startup costs of any business structure. It isn't a very common structure among small wine making businesses since there are shares of stocks involved.

Profits are taxed both at the corporate level and again when distributed to shareholders. When you structure a business at this level, there are often lawyers involved.

S CORPORATION

This is one of the most popular types of business entity people forms to it avoid double taxation. It is taxed similarly to a partnership entity. But an S Corp. needs to be approved to be classified as such, so it isn't very common among home based businesses

LIMITED LIABILITY COMPANY (LLC)

This is the most common business structure among most small and or home based businesses. It offers benefits for small businesses since it reduces the risk of losing all your personal assets in case you are faced with a lawsuit. It provides a clear separation between business and personal assets. You can also elect to be taxed as a corporation, which saves you money come tax time.

If you are unsure which specific business structure you should choose then, you can discuss it with an accountant. They will direct you in the best possible option for what your business goals are.

EIN NUMBER FROM IRS

EIN or Employer Identification number is essentially a social security or tax identification number but for your business. IRS and many other governmental agencies can identify your business via this unique 9 digit number.

Remember you will not need this number if you choose to be a sole proprietorship for your business.

It is simple to apply, either you can do it yourself or get your accountant to apply for you, but the process is simple, you fill out the form SS-4, which can be filed online, via Fax or via mail.

Here is a link to IRS website where you can download or fill out the form online.

https://www.irs.gov/businesses/small-businesses-self-employed/how-to-apply-for-an-ein

Form SS-4

Application for Employer Identification Number

Form **SS-4**
(Rev. January 2010)
Department of the Treasury
Internal Revenue Service

(For use by employers, corporations, partnerships, trusts, estates, churches, government agencies, Indian tribal entities, certain individuals, and others.)
► See separate instructions for each line.   ► Keep a copy for your records.

OMB No. 1545-0003

EIN

1 Legal name of entity (or individual) for whom the EIN is being requested	

Type or print clearly.

2 Trade name of business (if different from name on line 1)	**3** Executor, administrator, trustee, "care of" name	
4a Mailing address (room, apt., suite no. and street, or P.O. box)	**5a** Street address (if different) (Do not enter a P.O. box.)	
4b City, state, and ZIP code (if foreign, see instructions)	**5b** City, state, and ZIP code (if foreign, see instructions)	
6 County and state where principal business is located		
7a Name of responsible party	**7b** SSN, ITIN, or EIN	

8a Is this application for a limited liability company (LLC) (or a foreign equivalent)? ☐ Yes ☐ No
8b If 8a is "Yes," enter the number of LLC members ►

8c If 8a is "Yes," was the LLC organized in the United States? ☐ Yes ☐ No

9a Type of entity (check only one box). Caution. If 8a is "Yes," see the instructions for the correct box to check.

☐ Sole proprietor (SSN)
☐ Partnership
☐ Corporation (enter form number to be filed) ►
☐ Personal service corporation
☐ Church or church-controlled organization
☐ Other nonprofit organization (specify) ►
☐ Other (specify) ►

☐ Estate (SSN of decedent)
☐ Plan administrator (TIN)
☐ Trust (TIN of grantor)
☐ National Guard
☐ Farmers' cooperative
☐ REMIC
☐ State/local government
☐ Federal government/military
☐ Indian tribal governments/enterprises
Group Exemption Number (GEN) if any ►

9b If a corporation, name the state or foreign country (if applicable) where incorporated
State
Foreign country

10 Reason for applying (check only one box)
☐ Started new business (specify type) ►
☐ Hired employees (Check the box and see line 13.)
☐ Compliance with IRS withholding regulations
☐ Other (specify) ►

☐ Banking purpose (specify purpose) ►
☐ Changed type of organization (specify new type) ►
☐ Purchased going business
☐ Created a trust (specify type) ►
☐ Created a pension plan (specify type) ►

11 Date business started or acquired (month, day, year). See instructions.
12 Closing month of accounting year

13 Highest number of employees expected in the next 12 months (enter -0- if none).
If no employees expected, skip line 14.

Agricultural	Household	Other

14 If you expect your employment tax liability to be $1,000 or less in a full calendar year and want to file Form 944 annually instead of Forms 941 quarterly, check here. (Your employment tax liability generally will be $1,000 or less if you expect to pay $4,000 or less in total wages.) If you do not check this box, you must file Form 941 for every quarter. ☐

15 First date wages or annuities were paid (month, day, year). Note. If applicant is a withholding agent, enter date income will first be paid to nonresident alien (month, day, year) ►

16 Check one box that best describes the principal activity of your business. ☐ Health care & social assistance ☐ Wholesale-agent/broker
☐ Construction ☐ Rental & leasing ☐ Transportation & warehousing ☐ Accommodation & food service ☐ Wholesale-other ☐ Retail
☐ Real estate ☐ Manufacturing ☐ Finance & insurance ☐ Other (specify) ►

17 Indicate principal line of merchandise sold, specific construction work done, products produced, or services provided.

18 Has the applicant entity shown on line 1 ever applied for and received an EIN? ☐ Yes ☐ No
If "Yes," write previous EIN here ►

Third Party Designee	Complete this section only if you want to authorize the named individual to receive the entity's EIN and answer questions about the completion of this form.	
	Designee's name	Designee's telephone number (include area code)
	Address and ZIP code	Designee's fax number (include area code)

Under penalties of perjury, I declare that I have examined this application, and to the best of my knowledge and belief, it is true, correct, and complete.
Name and title (type or print clearly) ►

Applicant's telephone number (include area code)

Applicant's fax number (include area code)

OPENING A COMMERCIAL BANK ACCOUNT

This is one important step, but it can only be done after you have a fully executed article of incorporation which has been approved by the state, and you have an EIN number assigned by the IRS.

Once you have these two documents, you should be able to go to a bank and open your first commercial bank account.

But remember to check and understand various types of commercial checking account fees, you want to find a bank that offers free or almost free commercial checking account because some larger banks can charge you hundreds of dollars each month depending on how many transactions you do. Make sure to ask and shop around before you sign on the dotted line.

CHAPTER 21 - 5 BUSINESS MISTAKES TO AVOID

JUST as it is important to do the right things, it is just as important to learn from other's mistakes and know what to avoid when starting a wine making business. Consider five of the most common mistakes new wine making business owners make.

GETTING STARTED WITH NO EXPERIENCE

As with any small business, it is important that you have at least some experience before you get started. This means at least having experience doing it as a hobby or for personal wine giving. If you don't have any experience, take the time to take a class or read a book such as this then practice for a while to see if you are getting good at it. If you try to start a business with no experience than you are going to be taking a greater risk than you need to.

NO RESEARCH AND NO BUSINESS PLAN

A solid business plan built on lots of research is essential to any business success. Making wines as a hobby and selling a few is just a start, to turn it into a business you need to do some careful planning. You need to research bulk supplies and other business aspects.

You need to choose a name and register your business. There are a number of practical steps you need to take to start your business and having a thoroughly researched business plan will make sure you don't miss any of them.

NOT HAVING A PROPER WORKSPACE

If you are going to start a business from your home, you need to make sure you have the appropriate workspace available to accommodate the size of business you plan on running. For a wine making business, this means room to make and store the wine, enough storage for keeping all your supplies as well as some office space for your bookkeeping and sales.

The more room you have and the better organized you will be, and that would also mean your business will be more efficient and productive.

NOT FINDING A NICHE

If you are going to start a wine making business, you need to have a niche. If there is a particular type of wine you enjoy making and you're efficient in producing them, then you should place your focus there. There are a number of wine options, but you want to find one that not only sells well; but will also be easy for you to mass produce.

NOT HAVING A TARGET MARKET

It is important that you know where and how you plan to sell your wines once you get your business started. Many wine makers choose to use a website as a way to market and sell products, but there are other options as well. Let's actually take a look at some ways to promote and sell your wines to help you get some ideas.

CHAPTER 22 - PROMOTING YOUR WINES

YOU can't expect to sell wines and make a profit unless people know that your wines exist. There are many ways you can choose to promote your wines, and you don't need to use all of them. Rather you want to choose the best methods that will make people aware of your wines and be the friendliest option for your business budget. Let's take a look at your options.

ONLINE

In today's electronic focused society, perhaps the best option is to have an online presence. Having a website will allow you to appear on search engines and get attention from potential customers around the world who otherwise may not get a chance to find out about your wines.

If you are going to set up an online presence, the first thing you need to do is find a web host and create an account. For more professionalism, you should consider purchasing your own domain name before building your website (as I mentioned earlier).

Even without HTML knowledge, you can still create a decent website with the templates most web hosts offer, or you can hire a freelancer designer to put one together for you.

Once you have your website up, you should make sure you provide information on the wines you offer and include a portfolio of your wines so people can get a good idea of what you have to offer. Then you'll be ready to set up for accepting online sales. Here are few online freelance hire sites you can hire from:

99designs.com

Fiverr.com

Freelancer.com

Guru.com

Upwork.com

AN ONLINE STORE

With websites such as eBay and Etsy, it is easier than ever to sell handmade wines online. However, many of these options will deduct a percentage of the total sales so you may have to raise your prices. Another option is to set up an online store on your website and sell directly to customers.

A MAILING LIST

Once you have a website and start developing an online presence, you may want to consider starting a mailing list. This is a great way to get repeat customers since interested individuals can sign up for a mailing list. About once a month you can send out a newsletter showing your newest products and potentially a special discount to increase the incentive to purchase.

SOCIAL NETWORKING SITES

In my humble opinion, this is by far the best way to market your products. Before you build websites or even a domain name, you should focus on marketing on sites like Facebook. For me, Facebook provided the best results, and I believe it can do the same for you too. If you are like me and don't know how social media marketing works, then hire someone from one of those sites I mentioned and let them help you.

Once you see some success, then you should want to invest and get a website ready where you can display all your products and have shopping carts installed so people can buy directly from your site.

Customers want a way to contact sellers directly as well as a place where they can publicly express their shopping experiences. If you provide this, you will not only draw attention to your business, but you can also potentially increase sales. Keep in contact with your customers through networking sites such as Facebook and Twitter. Just remember to always include a link back to your website so people can find you easily.

PPC ADVERTISING

If simply having your items listed for sale online isn't doing enough, you can consider increasing some attention by buying PPC or pay per click advertising. You can do this through Google or other search engines.

As it sounds, this type of advertising means you only pay when someone actually comes to your website through a PPC link. You can often determine how much you pay and set a daily limit. This option isn't for everyone, but it is another online advertising option.

OFFLINE

Just because we live in an electronic and connected society, doesn't mean offline methods are no longer effective. Sometimes the best sales come from local areas and not worldwide sales. So be sure also to consider some offline methods of promotion to get your wines noticed.

BRANDING AND IDENTITY

Have some nice business cards printed that you can include with each purchase or simply to give out to people you meet every day. This can be an excellent way to get both new and repeat sales. It may be a good idea to have a nice logo designed to increase your promotions and have things look more professional.

LOCAL PAPERS AND FLYERS

If you can afford it, consider taking out an ad in the local newspaper. Another option that can be a little cheaper is to print some flyers and place them out around town in heavily frequented areas such as the local coffee shop, hair salons, grocery stores, beauty salons, etc. Anything you print should include your contact information and the web address (URL) of your online store.

COMMUNITY EVENTS

The best way to get local exposure is to sponsor events within the community. Offer to supply wines for events in exchange for a mention. This is a great place to start for a small wine making business. Get involved in various social gatherings that is how I got started and saw a great result.

INTRODUCTORY OFFERS

There are a lot of options when it comes to wines, and you need to give people a reason to choose yours over others. Competitive pricing is one option, but you can also offer special deals. Give a discount to first-time customers, holiday specials or clearance events for older stock. This way you get people interested, and you don't have to affect your profits long term by lowering your prices.

These are just some of the main options for promoting your wines. The methods of promotion are limited only by your imagination. Think of the various ways that may work for your company. Let's now take a look at some ways to sell your wines.

CHAPTER 23 - WHERE TO SELL YOUR WINES

ONE excellent way to both make a profit for your wine making business and increase your business exposure is to sell your wines to local wine stores. In addition to wine shops, you can also include liquor and beer stores and grocery stores that may specialize in locally made beer and wine.

RESEARCH POTENTIAL STORES

Before you approach any store make sure you do your research to ensure you are targeting the right locations and setting the right price point. Wine shops will often specialize in certain products, so you want to choose one that features merchandise that compliments your wines rather than detracts from them.

You also want to make sure that you are choosing wine shops with price points similar to what you expect to get for your wines.

HAVE A PROPOSAL

Before approaching wine shops make sure you have prepared a sales proposal. A great proposal is one that includes an overview of your wines including how they are made, what ingredients you use and the sizes, shapes, and flavors you create. Provide a description of how your wines are different from others.

Have a breakdown of price points for each size and outline how much inventory you have on hand or how quickly you can produce new bottles. You should have some samples and ask to meet with the shop owner or manager to discuss your product.

PITCH YOUR PROPOSAL

If possible, you want to visit wine stores in person so potential buyers can meet you. If you want to expand regionally then consider an eye-catching sales brochure with professional photos of your wines and have a website ready to show what you have to offer. Before spreading out be sure to do your research on a larger scale and find wine shops that meet your criteria in areas you are looking to expand. Offer to send samples and sales materials, so the store has a chance to get a first-hand look at what you have to offer.

GO TO TRADE SHOWS

Another good option is to consider setting up a vendor booth at a trade show. This can help provide you with exposure and allow you to meet with buyers from different retail outlets. If you can't afford a booth, you can at least attend a trade show and participate in networking events. This can help you develop new contacts that can eventually develop into new wine sales.

One thing that is sure to come up at some point is selling wholesale. Whether you are selling significant amounts to a single store or you get a larger contract to sell to a major retailer; you may eventually be asked to wholesale. Let's consider how you can do this to have the best potential outcome for your business.

SELLING WHOLESALE

Before you get asked to sell your wines wholesale, it is important that you do some research on the wholesale wine market. You can choose to sell wholesale directly to a buyer or through a wholesale distributor on a commission basis. When you work with a distributor, they will attend trade shows and make sales calls on your behalf so you can focus more of your time on the important part of making wines and efficiently running your company.

Start your research by considering the competition in retail stores. Take note of the price, shape, type and size of the competitions wines. Determine what makes your wines unique. Perhaps you use only organic ingredients, or your wines have an unusual color or design. There are a number of things that can make your wines stand out from the competition.

When it comes to pricing your wines for wholesale you want to price them at half retail price. Stores will often mark up their inventory by 100 percent over cost. For example, if you sell wholesale at $4 a wine, the retail store will likely charge $8 a wine.

It is important to consider exactly what it costs to produce your wines. You don't want the cost of making a wine to exceed 50 percent of your wholesale price. If it goes over 50 percent, then you need to either adjust your wholesale price higher or determine ways you can decrease your production costs.

Once you have a good idea of the appropriate wholesale price, you know what to quote a potential buyer.

Now that you have a good overview of making wines and starting your business you can choose to jump in and get some of the experience you need to get started. I've included some useful projects to help you get started. As you gain experience, you can expand on these projects or simply start experimenting on your own.

LAST WORDS

THE exciting world of wine-making is something worth looking into. You will be impressed at how well you can make wine when you put in a strong effort into the process.

I hope that this guide has helped you understand everything you need to do when getting started with wine-making on a budget. As you have noticed, it does not cost as much money to start making wine as you might think it would.

The process is not all that hard to handle either. It takes a while for your wine to be ready but after a while you will notice that your wine will stand out if prepared right.

Good luck with your efforts in making the best wines possible. You will be pleasantly surprised when you see just how well you can get a quality wine made in the comfort of your home.

I wanted to thank you for buying my book; I am neither a professional writer nor an author, but rather a person who always had the passion for making wine at home. In this book, I wanted to share my knowledge with you, as I know there are many people who share the same passion and drive as I do. So, this book is entirely dedicated to you.

Despite my best effort to make this book error free, if you happen to find any errors, I want to ask for your forgiveness ahead of time.

Just remember, my writing skills may not be best, but the knowledge I share here is pure and honest.

If you thought I added some value and shared some valuable information that you can use, please take a minute and post a review on wherever you bought this book from. This will mean the world to me. Thank you so much!!

Lastly, I wanted to thank my wife Jessica and my son Jacob for all their help and support throughout this book, without them, this book would not have been possible.

Thank you once again.

Cheers!

Made in the USA
Middletown, DE
23 July 2018